How to Be an

American in Italy

55
Insider Tips for Avoiding
Miscommunications, Misunderstandings,
and Embarrassing Faux Pas While
Visiting or Living in Italy

How to Be an

American in Italy

55
Insider Tips for Avoiding
Miscommunications, Misunderstandings,
and Embarrassing Faux Pas While
Visiting or Living in Italy

Jessica Scott Romano

For Daniele, the reason I was brave enough to become an American in Italy

Table of Contents

Introduction

Travel books about Italy are a dime a dozen. They are fun to look at with all their bright, colorful pictures, and they're useful, too, with all kinds of suggestions for where to go and what to see. But these books don't really give you an idea of what to expect when you arrive and start to live your daily life in Italy. They are for "tourists," and if you're like me, you want to be more than that, even if you're just here for a short time. You want to eat like the Italians eat, do the things they do, live like they live — or at least just not look silly in front of them.

I wrote this book because I wanted to give people something I would have loved to have had: specific advice about how to be an American living in or visiting Italy. It is one thing to come from another country in the European Union, where they use the same currency and the same type of measurement system and things of that nature, but it is a completely different (and sometimes culture-shocking) experience to come from America to Italy.

In America, over five thousand miles and an ocean away, most of the ideas we have about Italy come from Italian restaurants and television shows. But those aren't a true depiction of how it really is. What we think we know about Italy is often wrong, and there are so many new things we have to learn. And, more than that, we have to learn them in a way that is unique to us. Americans, in general, have a different way of thinking about and conceptualizing things (as does every other nationality, since your frame of reference depends on the environment you grew up in), so it helps to have someone like you "on the inside," who can help you see Italian things through an American lens and tell you about differences that would matter to you.

I have been traveling to Italy off and on for five years, always for three months at a time on a tourist visa, until early 2020, when I finally made the move here to live with my Italian pen-pal-turned-husband. I have been here for quite a while, but I am still learning new things every day, things that Italians take for granted because they have grown up with them. It's fun to take in all these new customs and try all these new things, but at times it is also kind of a lonely feeling to not always know how to act.

While it isn't a totally different world here and everyone understands that you aren't a native Italian and thusly won't know all their customs, it isn't fun to feel like an outsider or to keep worrying that you're going to make a mistake.

So, to help you feel more at home and more confident in your travels, I'm going to tell you all the things I wished I had known before moving to Italy, along with a few things that are just plain interesting. I cover foods and drinks (this section may be the most surprising: forget everything you knew about Italian pasta!), stereotypes, travel, home life, and even a few things you wouldn't expect you'd need to know about.

I am going to show you how to embrace your new Italian life — without losing your inner American.

This isn't one of those cold, heavily researched guides to the history of Italy, it isn't a list of tourist attractions you should visit before you die, and it obviously doesn't cover every aspect of Italian life and culture. These are simply fifty-five things I have personally observed and experienced, and I am sharing them with you because there is a high likelihood that you will experience them too.

Think of me less as a travel guide and more of a friend giving you advice. What you do with that advice is ultimately up to you, but surely you will be thankful you knew about a few of these things beforehand so you don't go looking for foods they don't have, get fined for throwing something in the wrong trash can, or goof up a first date by saying something you didn't know would be offensive!

Ready to take in all my hard-won wisdom? *Benissimo!* Let's get started.

Food and Drink

We start with the reason everyone is obsessed with Italy:
the food!

In the following two sections, I clear up some common
misconceptions about Italian meals and help you perfect your
table manners so you can be the best dinner guest you can be.

(Brace yourself, the spaghetti page is really going
to blow your mind!)

Part 1:
What's on My Plate?

Warning: The food in Italy may be a bit different than you are expecting.

Italy is known all over the world for its delicious cuisine, but there is a lot of "fake news" out there about what constitutes "Italian food."

Different ingredients, different flavors, different types of soda: I prepare you for it all so that you won't be surprised like I was.

1

Food Might Taste Different
Than You're Used To

You always hear about how delicious Italian food is, and this is one stereotype that is absolutely true. Italian food is some of the best food in the world, but the first time I came to Italy, I learned something surprising: it actually takes a bit of getting used to.

In America, it is assumed that more ingredients equal more flavor. Most spaghetti sauce has basil and oregano and garlic powder *and* parsley, and the list goes on and on. Here, it isn't about the quantity of ingredients, it is about the quality, and about how one ingredient brings out the flavor in another. So, for instance, the only dish you would ever see both basil *and* oregano in would be *caprese*, a simple salad-like dish with slices of tomatoes, mozzarella, and olive oil in addition to the spices. Otherwise, things are kept simple. Instead of just using salt to make a dish tastier, Italians use other spices that work together to bring out the natural flavor of the meat, pasta, etc. (and NEVER add salt at the table! This is a huge no-no).

I'm sure this makes sense on a cerebral level, but still, I was a bit disappointed when I had my first bite of genuine, bona fide, honest-to-goodness Italian pizza and found that it tasted like... well... nothing. It wasn't bad, it was just... bland. I was used to everything (especially things we consider to be "Italian," like pizza and pasta) being packed with all sorts of different flavors and spices and sauces in America, so I was expecting an explosion of flavory goodness! Instead, I was met with a feeling of extreme disappointment and, dare I say, something akin to doom. Was it possible that everyone was wrong about Italian food being the best?

Before you start to rethink your visit to the land of pasta-filled dreams, I will say that over the course of the next few days, my palate was slowly but surely cleansed of its American bias and I really started to be able to taste the true, mouthwatering flavor of the food. Italian food really *is* terrific after all, it is just a matter of getting used to the different style of cooking.

When it comes to Italian cuisine, less really is more, so don't get discouraged if you aren't a huge fan from the start. Just continue to eat as much as you can of as many dishes as you can as often as you can until you are able to appreciate the most subtle flavors, which I'm sure is a sacrifice you'll be willing to make.

2

Ingredients Are About to Get "Real"

Just as Italians use fewer ingredients to flavor their dishes, they also use fewer processed foods and additives. Processed foods are foods that are prepackaged and have been cooked, pasteurized, blanched, cut, dried, etc. before you buy them, and they often contain chemicals like preservatives that keep them fresher longer. There has been a heated debate about the nutritional value of foods like this, even in America, but I won't get into that here, as I am not a scientist and there are pros and cons on both sides.

What I will say instead is that, in Italy, most food is prepared from "real," fresh ingredients. No chemicals added. If a fruit or vegetable is not in season at the time, you'll have to wait around for the next harvest to see it in a dish again. Meat is hardly ever frozen and used later, it is often used the same day it is purchased from the butcher. And that meat is then seasoned with simple ingredients like salt, olive oil, or oregano, not with a shaker of steak seasoning like you might see in America (which is also delicious, don't get me wrong).

With the exception of a few prepackaged snacks like potato chips, you won't see anyone using garlic powder or onion powder: they use fresh garlic or fresh onions. Sauce for pasta and other dishes is typically made the day it is used, and hardly ever purchased pre-made in a can from the store.

Obviously, there are some exceptions to this rule, but in general, fresh ingredients are preferred, and even things that come pre-packaged lack the hard-to-pronounce preservatives you may be used to seeing on the label.

3

Expect to Experience Lower Blood Sugar

This one is going to be tough for travelers with a sweet tooth. In Italy, the sweets are much less sweet than they are in America. You may not always taste the difference, but if you look at the ingredients on, say, a package of Italian KitKat Bars, you will see that it contains significantly less sugar than its American counterpart.

Another thing that you won't see on that ingredients list is high-fructose corn syrup. This is a staple in many American snacks and drinks (and is fairly ubiquitous), but in Europe, it is actually highly restricted.

A lot of Americans who have been living in Italy for a while (who are often referred to as "expatriates" or, more commonly, "expats") admit that they sometimes miss the sugar rush-inducing versions of their favorite candies and snack cakes, but to them, I say the following: you're thinking about it all wrong.

There is a brand of chocolate chip cookie in Italy called Gocciole, and these drop-shaped *biscotti* are every bit as good as a good old American chocolate chip cookie. But, if you compare them to our Keebler brand chocolate chip cookies, for instance, you will see that one serving of Keebler Chips Deluxe cookies consists of two cookies and contains 9 grams of sugar, while a serving of the same number of Gocciole cookies only contains 5 grams of sugar. So, instead of missing the sugar rush, you should realize that this gives you the opportunity to eat double the amount of cookies! (Or to eat healthier and live longer and all that jazz...)

Note: Perhaps more jarring than going from American sweets to Italian ones is going in the opposite direction. If you stay in Italy for months and then celebrate your return to the U.S. with a big corner slice of cake piled high with icing and one of those pretty roses made of frosting, you're going to get a bellyache, big time. Trust me, I know. So pace yourself!

4

Your Morning Coffee
Won't Be the Same

Most Italians, like most Americans, love their coffee. The caffeine gets them going every morning and even sometimes helps them digest their lunch in the afternoon. But if you are expecting to see Italians walking around with big mugs of java like the ones we have in America, you are going to be sorely disappointed.

So-called (in Italy) "American-style coffee" is completely different than its Italian cousin. There are several types of Italian coffee, with the most popular being espresso, which is almost like a whiskey shot of coffee.

I was shocked the first time my husband ordered a *caffè* at a bar and was handed a teeny tiny cup that looked like it came from a toy tea party set. I started to get indignant on his behalf, thinking he was getting ripped off, but it turned out that that was exactly what he ordered. There is a lot of power (and a lot of flavor) in that tiny cup of coffee, perhaps even more than in the big American version you are used to!

Another note about coffee is that, from what I've seen, most Italians like their coffee "black," with no cream or sugar added (I actually tried adding sugar to espresso once and found that this rendered it undrinkable. But that's just me!). There are a few exceptions, though, my favorite being *caffè latte* or, "milk with coffee." Here is a quick guide to some of the most popular coffees in Italy:

- *espresso* - Espresso is a small but caffeine-packed cup of coffee with a strong flavor and a bit of *crema*, which in this case is like a thick, fluffy foam. You can get it at a bar or restaurant, or you can make it at home with a coffee machine or on the stove. It's usually served with breakfast and/or after meals.
- *moka* - Moka is almost the same as espresso, but its flavor is a bit less intense. It doesn't have the *crema* that a good espresso has, but it still has a nice taste. It's called Moka because you make it on the stove in a little, single-serve coffee maker called a Moka Pot that looks a bit like an old-timey metal teapot.
- *caffè macchiato* - Now we're starting to get into the coffees for people who find black coffee a bit too strong. *Caffè macchiato* is espresso with just a drop or two of milk added to bring down the intensity of the *caffè* without losing its rich flavor.
- *cappuccino* - You have probably heard of this one. Cappuccino is the fancy coffee that comes in a bigger cup with lots of steamed milk foam. This is the coffee that people put designs in like hearts and flowers.
- *caffè latte* - This one isn't always considered sophisticated or fancy, but it's my favorite, so I'm including it on the list! *Caffè latte* is milk with coffee. Basically, you take an espresso, pour it in a glass, then

fill the rest of the glass with milk (at home you can even just use milk from the fridge or warm it up on the stove). It's perfect for dunking cookies in at breakfast, and it helps to quench that thirst you get when you first wake up in the morning moreso than plain espresso does.

- **caffè corretto** - Now for a coffee you probably shouldn't drink in the morning. *Caffè corretto* is espresso with liquor added (just a bit though, don't overdo it or it's just gross). Typically that liquor is something like grappa or brandy, but I personally recommend you try it with Bailey's Irish Cream (you can thank me later!).
- **caffè lungo** and **caffè corto** - Italian for "long coffee," *caffè lungo* is typically coffee made with more water, and *caffè corto* is "short coffee," and is made with less water. They both have around the same level of caffeine, but the former is more diluted while the latter has a stronger coffee taste.

I have to admit that, in America, I wasn't a huge coffee drinker. When I came to Italy, though, I started to appreciate it, mostly due to the fact that it is such a big part of Italians' daily routine. It is customary to have coffee in the morning with breakfast (and maybe again with a second breakfast) and typically after another meal during the day. This is something you do with family or friends. It isn't just about the coffee, it is about sitting down with the people you care about and taking a short pause to just chat and spend time together.

So while at first coffee was a bit strong for me (until I

discovered my beloved *caffè latte*!), the camaraderie of the experience made me give it more of a chance. Even if you aren't a coffee convert, though, your hosts/guests will still be more than happy to have you just sit and chat and keep them company while they drink theirs!

5

Foods You Shouldn't Look for Because They're Not Really Italian

America is full of Italian restaurants. We Americans are crazy for Italian cuisine! But what you may not know is that the "Italian" in both of the preceding sentences should always be surrounded by quotation marks, because a lot of the foods we think are Italian are actually not Italian at all. They are actually just dishes that were *inspired* by Italian food and altered for an American clientele.

Here are just a few examples (get ready to have your reality shattered):

- **garlic bread** - Italians love garlic and they love bread, but the delicious, buttery, garlicy goodness that we serve alongside our best pasta dishes is actually not an Italian invention at all. They don't eat garlic bread here, and they will be very confused if you ask for it (believe me, I've tried).
- **breadsticks** - Along the same lines, breadsticks as we know them in America do not exist in Italy. They *do* have breadsticks of their own, but they are crunchier and dryer, not soft and fluffy on the inside like the ones we get when we order take-out pizza or eat at

Olive Garden.

- **Fettuccine Alfredo** - This one was a big shock to me. While Fettuccine Alfredo as we know it really was invented in Rome (by a chef who wanted to encourage his wife to eat more after she had their first baby, which is adorable), Italians don't really eat this buttery, cheesy dish today. Some, like my husband, have never even heard of it! But if you want a close approximation of what we think of as Fettuccine Alfredo, ask for *fettuccine al burro* (fettuccine with butter).

- **Chicken Parmesan** - Okay, we know that Italians are responsible for Parmesan cheese (and they are very particular about it, as you will see later in this section), and we know that they eat chicken. But what most Americans *don't* know is that the dish we call Chicken Parmesan, with the chicken smothered in sauce and cheesy deliciousness, usually placed carefully on a bed of pasta? That basically amounts to blasphemy here. Chicken and pasta are *never, ever* eaten on the same plate. You can have a pasta dish, then a chicken dish, but never together. So all those recipes you see in cookbooks or on the internet for "Italian chicken pasta" in whatever form and combination are not truly Italian at all. Even if they taste good, there is nothing authentic about them. Sad, I know.

6

SPAGHETTI AND MEATBALLS
ARE NOT A THING!!!

This may be the most shocking, most upsetting thing you read in this entire book. But it's better that you hear it from a friend than from someone else:

Italians do not eat spaghetti and meatballs.

Before you slam down the book and call me a liar, just bear with me. Italians eat spaghetti and they eat meatballs, but they never eat them together. In fact, I made this a separate entry on the list just to help you remember that these two things are always kept on separate dishes.

There are a few types of pasta that are served with a meat *sauce*, but never meat*balls*. Why? I haven't been able to find a clear answer.

The only time I have ever eaten spaghetti and meatballs in Italy was when my husband made me a special dish to remind me of home (and then told me never to expect to see that dish outside of our apartment). But I can guarantee you that if you ask any American to name an Italian dish, almost every single person will say spaghetti and meatballs. So maybe we need to start spreading the truth around a bit so no one will be disappointed!

7

There Are a Lot of Dishes Italians Think Are American... but They're Not

Just like there are tons of foods we think are Italian but aren't, Italians have some mistaken ideas about our menu too.

Take "patate americane," for example. These medallion-cut "American potatoes" are golden, fried, and a bit sweet (but not sweet enough to be equivalent to what we would refer to as "sweet potatoes") and they are incredibly tasty. But they aren't "American." I don't even think we have the type of potatoes they use to make them in our country!

And while I can forgive them that mistake in potato attribution, this brings me to the one and only thing about Italy that gets me fired up: "*pizza americana*."

In Italy, "*pizza americana*," or "American-style pizza," is pizza covered in hot dogs and french fries. Have you ever had pizza like that in the States? I haven't! And, just as Italians may get offended that someone could think that all they eat is spaghetti and meatballs, Americans (or is it just me?) may also get offended when they realize that Italians think that all *we* ever eat are hot dogs and french fries. Sure, it's hard to find someone who doesn't like those things, but that's not *all* we eat. And we surely don't eat them on pizza!!!

Alright, maybe it's best if we move on...

8

The Pizza Is Completely Different

Are we still talking about pizza? Ugh... okay.

Putting the so-called "*pizza americana*" aside, we now have to discuss the difference between actual *pizza americana* — pizza you would eat in America — and *pizza italiana*.

Since Italy is the birthplace of pizza, obviously this is one of the best dishes you can get there. But, if you are used to American pizza, you may be a bit confused or even disappointed at first, because the style and the taste are so different.

In America, pizza typically has a thicker crust than it does in Italy, and much more sauce. That sauce also has more spices in it (and usually so does the crust). In Italy, the pizza base is simpler: just a bit of tomato sauce on a thinner, plain crust.

Italians also use different pizza toppings, like buffalo cheese, eggplants, potatoes, tuna, bell peppers, or salami.

Note: One thing you should really, definitely make a note of is that in Italy, they don't have what we call "pepperoni." In the U.S., those spicy disks of meat are my favorite pizza topping, but I quickly found out that if you ask for a pizza with pepperoni here, you get a pizza covered in bell peppers!

9

Desserts Are Different Too

If there is one food category in which Americans really shine, it is desserts. We have gorgeous, three-tiered cakes frosted to perfection. We have soft, gooey chocolate chip cookies. We have brownies, we have blondies, we have puddings and ice cream cakes and pie. I'm getting hungry just thinking about it!

Italians have some of these things, but, like most everything else, they put their own spin on it. As I already told you, Italy's sweet treats are usually a lot less sweet than ours, but there are other key differences as well.

For example, most cakes don't come with icing. At most, they will have a sprinkle of powdered sugar or a dollop of whipped cream and fruit on top, but usually your average, everyday cake here looks naked to us. Icing-less cake is good in its own way, but if you're used to frosting, you're going to have to eat a lot of Italian cake before you stop feeling like it's missing something.

Cookies are another thing that may throw you. In America, we like soft, moist cookies, but in Italy, most cookies are expected to be crunchy. Sometimes this is because they are baked twice (which is where the word "*biscotti*", meaning "twice-cooked" comes from), but usually, it is just how they are. Again, they are not bad at all (in fact, they're pretty delicious), it is just that Italians have a totally different style of baking cookies than we do.

Even things like hot chocolate are different: in America, hot chocolate is thinner, almost like warm chocolate milk or at most a thin milkshake, but in Italy, it is closer to a pudding. You eat it with a spoon, and don't expect it to come from a powder. It is always made with melted chocolate, milk, sugar, and a bit of cornstarch to thicken it up.

10

Milk Doesn't
Always Go in the Fridge

This one blew my mind.

In America, if you want to buy milk, you head to the refrigerated section of the grocery store. In Italy, you head to one of the regular old room-temperature aisles. While there are some brands of milk that come in a (much-smaller-than-we're-used-to) plastic bottle in the dairy aisle, the majority of Italians drink milk that comes in a carton called a Tetra Pak.

This milk can be kept on a shelf or in a cabinet for months before you open it because it has been processed with Ultra High-Temperature Pasteurization (UHT). This process of heating the milk to an extremely high temperature for a few seconds kills more bacteria than normal pasteurization and results in milk that is "shelf-stable," as long as it comes in the Tetra Pak, which has been sterilized before use.

Once you open a box of milk (which is weird to say...), you have to put it in the fridge and drink it within a week or less, which is something that makes more sense to us!

11

Fruit Juice Must Actually Contain...
Well, Fruit Juice

I can't tell you how many times I have bought fruit juice in America, only to check the label and see that it only contains something like one percent real fruit juice. The rest is sugar and a bunch of artificial flavors, which kind of defeats the purpose of trying to be healthy and drink fruit juice in the first place.

In Italy, fruit juice was once required to contain at least 12 percent real fruit if you wanted to call it "fruit juice." Since 2018, that percentage has been raised to a whopping 20 percent. While this still might not sound like enough to classify something as "fruit juice," just know this: in America, there is no such rule that I have found. Instead, the law only says that it must be written on the package that "this product contains less than 1% juice" or something similar in order to be called "fruit juice."

Some manufacturers get around this by calling it something like a "fruit drink," but in reality, these things should really all just be called "fruit-*flavored* drinks," because they are made to taste like fruit without actually containing much fruit at all.

12

Soft Drinks May Surprise You

Piggybacking off of my last point, I want to tell you about an experience I had the first time I came to Italy. My future husband and I were at a restaurant, and we were ordering soft drinks to go with our pizza. I saw that there was orange Fanta on the menu, and I thought "Oh, thank goodness! A soft drink I'm familiar with!" So I ordered the Fanta (a brand that actually originated in Naples, Italy, by the way) and waited for my bright orange, sugary, flavor-packed beverage to arrive. What came to my table, though, was a cup full of some yellowish, almost pulpy sort of liquid that smelled as different from my beloved Fanta as it looked.

The contrast was so jarring that I thought they had gotten my order wrong, but my husband assured me that that was, indeed, orange Fanta. He even took a drink and confirmed that it was the same orange Fanta he had been drinking in Italy his whole life. Unconvinced, I took a sip... and I swear it just tasted like carbonated orange juice.

The reason for this is that, just like you can't say that a drink is a fruit juice in Italy if it doesn't contain actual fruit, you can't say that a beverage is "orange" unless it is made with actual oranges. The difference between the two Fantas is that the orange taste I love in America is produced with artificial flavors. We looked up the ingredients, and I was shocked to see that there are actually, genuinely, no real oranges in orange Fanta at all, unless that is included in what the ingredients list refers to as simply "natural flavors." Which is why, if you look closely, they always refer to it as an "orange-flavored" drink on the label. The Italian one, on the other hand, is made with real fruit.

After this disappointment, I started noticing more differences in the soft drinks, such as that Sprite and Coca-Cola taste a bit different due to the lack of high-fructose corn syrup (and the fact that the former might actually contain real lemons and limes). This isn't a huge deal, but I wish someone had told me beforehand, so I would have been prepared for the change!

You should also be aware that Diet Coke and other diet sodas don't really exist here. Instead, there are some soft drinks that are called "light" or "zero," but these sometimes still contain real sugar along with the artificial sweeteners, so people with diabetes and similar conditions should be extra cautious with them.

Another good tip is that, if you see a soft drink called "Ginger," do not assume it is the same as Ginger Ale!! In Italy, Ginger is a bright red drink made with a whole bunch of real, natural ginger — something we as Americans are not used to at all after drinking something like Canada Dry Ginger Ale, which contains a negligible (and unspecified) amount of real ginger and has been severely diluted. Ginger soda, on the other hand, is very strong and kind of bitter.

On a less confusing final note, Italy has its own soft drink brands that some of us have never heard of, such as Chinotto, which is a bittersweet drink that looks like Coke but is flavored with fruit from a special type of orange tree. Another biggie is Schweppes, which actually comes from neighboring Switzerland, but is one of my favorites. I highly recommend the lemon kind!

13
Obey the Cheese Rules

Americans love cheese. An extra cheesy cheeseburger, dripping with cheese? Macaroni and cheese? Cheese pizza? Cheesecake? Yes, yes, yes, and yes.

Italians love cheese too — they have entire aisles dedicated to it at the grocery store and so many different types and variations that it would take you months to try them all. Italy is like cheese Heaven... but, just like real Heaven, there are a few rules a cheese has to follow to get in.

First, there is no such thing as "American cheese" here. Those pre-cut slices you use for grilled cheese sandwiches or for making burgers at home don't exist (at least not in the flavor we're used to). But this is not because Italians are discriminating against American products in general. It is because in Italy, what we call American cheese (and use every day without giving it a second thought...) doesn't meet the high standards they set for cheese production. Similar to a lot of American fruit drinks, it is considered to be a "cheese *product*" instead of actual cheese because it is made in a different way (with powdered milk, for example), and is not certified with an official seal declaring which region's cows produced it.

There is not much cheddar in Italy either, but you may find it on a burger in places like McDonald's or Burger King.

Another rule I was not aware of is that, apparently, what we refer to in America as "Parmesan cheese" is not actually Parmesan cheese at all. In Italy, you absolutely, positively cannot call a cheese Parmesan (actually, it's Parmigiano-Reggiano, if you want to get technical) unless it is produced by a company that is a member of the *Consorzio del Formaggio Parmigiano-Reggiano* or "Parmigiano-Reggiano Cheese Consortium." In order for a cheese to be true, certified Parmigiano Reggiano, the milk used to produce it must come from certain cows who eat a certain diet, and it must be submitted to certain processes and checks before being aged for at least twelve months (and up to thirty-six months).

In Europe, you can get into serious legal trouble for calling a cheese Parmesan when it isn't, and in recent years they have really been cracking down on this... and they probably should, even in America. According to the Food and Drug Administration, almost a quarter of all so-called "100% Grated Parmesan Cheese" bought in America is not only *NOT PARMESAN AT ALL*, but actually contains anywhere from three to ten percent cellulose. Or, to put it in plainer English, wood pulp.

There's nothing tastier than lies, right?

14

McDonald's May Not Remind You of Home

I don't know about everyone else who moves away from America, but from time to time, even here in food paradise, I get an almost overwhelming hankering for a good, greasy, fast-food burger. Luckily, there are plenty of McDonald's, Burger King, and even KFC restaurants here... but perhaps a bit unluckily, the food there doesn't taste the same.

As I alluded to before, Italian food has to follow some really strict guidelines in order to be sold. There is actually an entire law enforcement department dedicated to checking food- and pharmaceutical-related infractions: the *Nucleo Anti Sofisticazioni* or NAS, which was established in 1962. And, to be quite honest, American ingredients don't always make the cut, especially the meat.

Here in Italy, the meat used in burgers is of a higher quality and is produced in certain (local) places where it can be monitored from beginning to end, so those who use it know exactly what they're getting. This isn't cheap, so the burgers cost a bit more than you're used to back home.

The cheese is also slightly different (although, like I said, I am pretty sure cheddar is allowed), as are the types of side dishes. You won't find coleslaw or macaroni and cheese at KFC, but you may find a different selection of side items like *crocchette di patate*, which are basically big, fried tater tots with mashed potatoes inside. You may also find different entrees and different desserts, the latter of which are sometimes pretty spectacular.

In large part, this change is due to the fact that Italians themselves have different ideas about what constitutes a meal, and the restaurants have to adapt to that style, even if they still have roots in America.

Part 11:
At the Table

Now that I told you *what* you'll be eating, I'm going to give you some tips on *how* to eat it and serve it so you don't look out of place at the *tavolo da pranzo* (lunch table).

This advice will save you a lot of embarrassment... and maybe even save a life or two!

15

Pace Yourself

One of the biggest mistakes I made on my first trip to Italy happened when I went to my then-future in-laws' house for a meal. They put a big plate full of delicious food down in front of me and I ate it all right up. It was delicious, and my stomach was stuffed and happy. I was more than content to sit there and digest in the pleasant company for the next hour or so, but then my husband told me something that changed everything:

That was just the appetizer.

In America, most meals are served with the main course and the side dishes all on one plate. But in Italy, the first plate is just the beginning. If you are eating a meal with others (especially lunch), even on an average day there are usually at least three or four separate courses. Appetizers are usually just for special occasions, but there is always *il primo* (the first dish), usually consisting of pasta or risotto, followed by *il secondo* (the second dish), which is typically meat or fish, sometimes with a small salad as well. Next comes the fruit course, then the one that you will always wish you had left more space for dessert (which may or may not include coffee or something alcoholic to help you digest everything).

In Italy, there is one food per plate, and each one gets its own course. This is a perfectly fine way to eat, but it does take some preparation. Italians in general tend to eat more than Americans (and they hardly ever gain weight, grr...), so each course consists of what most Americans would consider to be a full-fledged meal. My advice is to not fill up on the first course so that you have some room left for the other courses because it is all food worth trying!

Note: If you are living with just your spouse or one roommate or relative, you typically forego all the extra courses and just have *il primo* for lunch, since it's more casual. But if you are visiting with family or friends, you can expect them to pull out all the stops, so plan accordingly.

16

There *Has* to Be a Tablecloth...

For the most part, we never had much use for a tablecloth at my house growing up, so I had no idea that they were so essential to the household in Italy. For every meal, there *must* be a tablecloth on the table. Heck, my mother-in-law even puts one down when we have a quick afternoon snack! The tablecloth "rule" is one you cannot break, even if you're not having a big family meal. No one is going to get mad if you don't use one at your own house (although they may judge you), but I can tell you from experience that if you try to start eating without one at someone else's house, you can expect a lot of fretting and having to lift up your plate while someone whips out a tablecloth and covers the table.

Once the meal is finished, whoever is in charge will scoop up the tablecloth and take it outside, where they shake out the crumbs in the yard or over the balcony (unless you live in an apartment, in which case you shake them out onto the floor and sweep them up). Then, if it's not stained, you fold it up and put it back in the drawer for the next meal. Or snack. Or random cookie...

17

...but It's for a Good Reason

There are surely many reasons why a tablecloth is such a staple. It protects the table from spills. It looks nice. It makes things feel "civilized" and "fancy." But there is one reason that takes precedence above all other reasons in my heart and many others': the bread.

Bread is something that no meal in Italy can go without. There is always bread on the table and it is always fresh (if you're thinking about that bag of square-shaped sandwich bread in your cabinet right now, think again: hardly anyone eats that here). Many Italians go to the *panetteria* to get bread every day. Some even have fresh bread delivered to their door every morning!

And when you are eating that bread, you keep it on the table, not on a plate, which is why you need the tablecloth. Now it all makes sense!

This is a strangely important thing to keep in mind for us Americans. Back home, I would always keep my rolls and biscuits or other bread items on the edge of my plate, but when I tried to do that here once to keep things clean and tidy, I received some very shocked, almost scandalized looks from the other dinner participants. After dinner was over, my husband explained this bread "rule" to me, and now I am explaining it to you (ahead of time, which I personally would have appreciated...) so you don't make that particular faux pas.

18

Never Bring Peeled Fruit
to the Table

This is something I never would have thought about before, and only learned recently when my husband and I hosted our first guest in our new apartment and I made what was apparently another pretty big mistake.

My first time as an Italian wife/hostess was going really well: the lasagna we had made was a huge hit and our guest ate so many of my appetizers that I wasn't sure he was going to have room for the main course. Everything was perfect... until I went to the kitchen to get the pears for the fruit course. I was in there for a bit, washing and peeling them carefully and cutting them into what I thought were some pretty sophisticated-looking slices, but then my husband came in and whispered, "Wait, don't peel... oh."

At this point I was already arranging the peeled fruit on a plate, thinking I had done a pretty great job, if I did say so myself. But then I heard my husband tell our guest (in a somewhat embarrassed tone) that he was sorry, that I had gone ahead and peeled the pears, after which they both started giggling (I dare say it was more of a guffaw!).

Obviously, I was very confused... isn't it more polite to serve guests prepared fruit instead of just handing them a pear? Apparently, the answer is no!

In Italy, they told me, it is customary to bring the fruit to the table washed, but not peeled (unless we're talking about something like *fichi di india*, which are hard to peel because they're covered in prickly thorns). So, if you are serving pears, peaches, apples, oranges, etc., you give your dinner guests a knife, but let them peel their own fruit. Otherwise, be prepared for everyone to keep teasing you about it for the rest of the day!

19

Never Cross Arms
When Clinking Glasses

This one is another biggie, but for a different reason.

If you are in a situation that involves a toast or a "cheers" or a "*salute*," you have to clink your glass against everyone else's glass. But, in the process of doing that, you have to be very careful not to cross arms with anyone else. There is an old superstition that this brings bad luck to the arm-crossers. Most people laugh at this now but prefer not to do it anyway, just in case.

As with every superstition, the validity of the belief is up for debate. I *can* say, however, that the one and only time I ever crossed arms with someone during a toast, the someone I crossed arms with ended up in the hospital with a heart attack a few days later. Coincidence? Maybe. But will I ever cross arms during a toast again? Definitely not!!

20

Italians Always Eat Together

There are many American families that eat dinner together every night. No matter where everyone goes during the day, everyone usually sits down together for at least one family meal before the day is through. Italians, though, take this to another level. They eat breakfast together, lunch together (unless someone is at work), snacks together, dinner together: every meal is eaten together at the table. If someone is late getting home from work, they wait until they arrive to eat. If someone has to get up early to go on a trip, everyone else gets up early to eat breakfast with them.

It is a very sweet tradition, but there are many Americans that will find this a tiny bit claustrophobic. Some people are used to eating dinner on their own when they get home from work or in their rooms while they're studying or when they have a break in whatever they're doing, so meals can feel like more of a "big deal" here, especially if you are going to be a bit late and they insist on holding dinner for you (which, to me, as an introvert and overly polite person, is kind of mortifying. I hate putting people out!).

Like most aspects of Italian culture, though, it is about family and spending time together, so we can appreciate the gesture.

21

Be Prepared for Longer Meals

As we have already established, Italian food is great, so it makes sense that you'd want to linger over it at the table. You may be surprised, though, at how much longer meals last in Italy than they do in the States.

Since there are more courses to get through and since everyone is at the table together, meals like lunch and dinner tend to last upwards of an hour (if not three or four if it's a special occasion). We Americans have a tendency to want to eat and leave, but you can't do that in Italy without looking rude. Italians have some of their best conversations over their finished dinner plates, and meals are a time to connect and bond with each other.

So, settle in and enjoy the food and the amicable atmosphere, because you may be there a while. But it's a great opportunity to get to know people better, and to practice your Italian language skills!

Daily Life

What? There's more to life than just eating?
Alright, if you say so...

The next three sections address things you will
come across every day inside Italian houses and outside on
the winding streets.

Whether you prefer going out or staying in, I've got all the
tips you need.

Part 1:

Around the House

A house is a house is a house. Right? Not necessarily.

While the bulk of the things you'd find or do inside an Italian house are undoubtedly the same as you'd find your own house in America, there are a few key differences you should know before you go (especially if you want to avoid burnt cakes and burnt apartment buildings).

22

Meet the Metric System

Cups, teaspoons, Fahrenheit, pounds — forget it all. Italy (and most of the rest of the world) uses the Metric System instead of the Imperial one for measuring. To be honest, once the Metric System was explained to me, it made a heck of a lot more sense than the Imperial System, since everything is based on tens. In fact, I wondered why we haven't just been using that one ourselves this whole time... but that doesn't mean I know how to make it work for me yet.

In all honesty, this is going to be one of the hardest things to learn if you stay in Italy for an extended period of time. For us Americans, there is no real way to conceptualize what one kilogram of pasta or 16 degrees Celsius feels like because we aren't used to thinking in those terms. Instead of cups or teaspoons or ounces, they use grams or milliliters. Instead of pounds they use kilograms to weigh things. Instead of Fahrenheit, they use Celsius for temperature. If you don't take this last one into account, you can get into some real trouble when it comes to the outfit you choose in the morning or what temperature to put the oven on when you're baking.

My husband's advice is to stop trying to do conversions every time you want to know what the temperature is outside. Instead, learn like you did when you were a child. When it's ten degrees Celsius, for example, go outside and see what it feels like. It's chilly, right? So now you have an idea of where to start. If you do this enough times, you will start to get a feel for what the numbers mean, and you don't have to keep trying to translate the Celsius temperature to Fahrenheit every time you want to know if you need a jacket or not.

The same goes for weight: if you don't know how heavy one kilogram is, go and find something with that weight written on it and pick it up. One of the easiest ways to do this is with packages of pasta, which usually weigh 500 grams (so you'd need two for this experiment), but you can use anything, as long as you know its weight.

The measuring of ingredients in the kitchen is much simpler, though. Most Italians have a scale you can use to measure dry ingredients in grams or kilograms, and they have a measuring cup for wet ingredients that tells you the amount in milliliters.

This stuff is actually all simpler in a way, we just have to adjust to it!

23

Check Before You Plug Something in

Most travelers find this out beforehand, but I'll repeat it anyway because it can be a pretty big problem if you don't. In Italy, both the electrical outlets and the voltage they provide are different than in the U.S., so if you bring any appliances like hair dryers or straighteners or blenders, they may not work here.

In America, the voltage coming through our electrical sockets is 120 volts, but in Italy, it's 230. So if you plug something in that can only handle the former, it's going to get fried. Luckily, a lot of stores sell what they call "dual-voltage" appliances, and these can work for both voltage levels (even more luckily, most laptops and phones are already dual-voltage). Just check the label or manual to make sure before you plug it in!

In order to plug *anything* in, though, you're going to have to invest a couple dollars in some adapters. In the U.S., plugs have straight, squarish ends, but in Italy, the prongs on plugs are rounded. To be technical, there are three types of plugs in Italy: C, F, and L. America uses A and B. But in order to convert an A or B to a C, F, or L, you just have to pop an adapter on over the prongs and plug it in — after checking that the appliance is compatible with the voltage, of course.

24

No Plastic, Please

In Italy, they take conserving the environment and reducing pollution/waste very seriously. In most other countries, they just talk about doing better for the world, but in Italy, they actually do. There are a number of environmental laws and, unlike some places in America, there are no two ways of thinking about it: everyone has to take those three Rs we learned in school (reduce, reuse, and recycle) and actually put them into practice, or else they get in big trouble.

This is why you will rarely find any plastic packaging on food or other items. Most things are wrapped in biodegradable packages, and the large majority of people have reusable bags to carry their groceries in when they go to the store. They are phasing out everything from cellophane wrappers to plastic tops on restaurant cups to straws because these things just end up as waste that can end up in the sea, where it can choke and kill poor turtles or other wildlife.

You are also expected to properly recycle the plastic things you *do* buy, otherwise you can get fined. Which brings me to the next vital thing you need to know...

25

The Trash Can Be a Bit Confusing

In America, we typically have two types of waste: garbage and recycling, the latter of which is then sometimes divided a bit further to make things easier. When you're out and about, there is usually one trash can for everything, and at home it is usually more or less the same. Tissues, apple peels, old sponges, tape: it all goes into the same trash can.

Not in Italy.

In Italy, there are six different types of trash, and you are expected to keep them separate or you can actually get into some serious legal trouble. Here is a list to help you keep them straight:

- **umido (humid)** - Also known as *organico*, or "organic" trash, this is typically biodegradable or food-related trash like fruit peels, coffee grounds, fingernails, and pasta you dropped on the floor and can't eat because there's cat hair on it. These things are collected and turned into compost, which is later reused to grow plants, which is pretty cool.
- **indifferenziato (indifferent)** - Otherwise known as "mixed" trash, this one is for everything that doesn't

fit into any other category. Some examples include used paper towels, tissue paper, clothing tags, sponges, microfiber fabric, doll hair, etc.

- *vetro* (glass) - This is for bottles, broken mirrors, vases, windows — anything made of glass.

- *plastica* (plastic) - While they may not use it as often as we do, there is still plastic in Italy, and when you dispose of it, you put it here. Plastic beverage bottles, plastic gelato tubs, plastic cutlery, plastic food wrappers, plastic bags, those tiny plastic string things that pin socks to the cardboard package they come in, they all belong here.

- *carta* (paper) - This one would be self-explanatory... except sometimes things are considered paper when you wouldn't think they would be. You can put books, pieces of notepaper, cardboard, newspaper, and other things of that nature in the paper trash, but you can also sometimes put the shiny or plasticky-feeling packages from cookies or ice cream or milk (those Tetra Paks I told you about) in there too, so you have to check the packaging carefully.

- **electronics/batteries** - In America, if an AA or AAA battery dies, you just pitch it in the trash can. In Italy, though, this is a crime! Anything electronic including computers, phones, DVD players, and even batteries all have to be taken to a specially designated dump. Then they are recycled and turned into new electronic devices, so it's like the circle of life!

In every case, before you throw anything away, check the label on it. There is almost always a little symbol near the bar code or the ingredients list that will let you know which type of trash it is, so you can dispose of it properly.

You should also check the rules in your particular town before you take out the trash, because sometimes each community has different rules about what goes where. For example, when my husband lived in another town, the aluminum foil went in the glass recycling bin, but in our current town, you recycle it with the plastic. Luckily, it is usually pretty easy to find these rules online as each town has its own website. They also send out a mailer a couple times a year with the list of what to throw away where, along with a calendar so you can keep track of which days to throw it.

Part 11:
Out and About

Whether you're hitting the streets for a sightseeing trip or just heading to work, here's how to get where you're going, what you'll see on the way, and what to do when you get there so you don't stick out like a sore American thumb.

26

Italy Is a Safe Place

This item might be a bit prickly for some readers. But as of the time of writing (late 2020), America isn't a very peaceful place. While this isn't true of every city, town, or neighborhood, it *is* true that, in general, we have issues with violence, crime, and even terrorism. Too many families know someone who has been affected by these things in some way, and we have all seen too many stories on the news about violent protests gone awry and school shootings that took the lives of far too many young people.

Italy isn't like that. If you look up any study that compares crime statistics between the two countries, you will see that Italy has significantly less violent crime than America, and actually has a much lower crime rate in general, even compared to its own past rates. Obviously, crime and violence happen everywhere, but in Italy, you don't have to be *quite* so worried about certain things when you are out walking, especially if you're not in one of the main tourist areas like Rome or Venice.

The reason I bring this up is that, as an American, I didn't realize how much a sort of American-grown hyper-vigilance was ingrained in me until one day when my husband and I were visiting a park with his brother and our seven-year-old nephew. The nephew was scrambling up the monkey bars, showing us how high he could climb, when suddenly another little boy appeared to my left. I glanced over just in time to see him raise what appeared to be a small but very real gun. It was black with a brown handle, and glinted menacingly in the sun, warning of what was to come.

I panicked as he raised said gun and pointed it at our nephew, and all I could think was "Oh no, it's happening! A shooting! I have to stop him before he shoots my nephew!"

Filled with dread, knowing I was already too late, I started to reach out... then I heard the plasticky click of the trigger of an obviously fake gun.

My husband and brother-in-law laughed when I let out an explosive sigh of relief and joked "It's okay, Jessica, this isn't America. Not everyone has a gun!" It was funny (and they still tease me about it to this day), but my overreaction led me to realize that there really are some deeply embedded ideas/coping mechanisms/fears we bring with us even when we leave America, and this is something that sets us apart from our Italian hosts. Whereas most Italians' first impression would have been that the gun was a toy, that a man walking toward a woman on the street *isn't* a rapist but just a normal guy, and that an angry person charging into a store *wouldn't* be armed and ready to take out everyone around him instead of just asking to see the manager, these are the kind of instinctual, gut reactions that some of us as Americans have developed in recent years.

So, while I am not telling you to let your guard down or walk around in dark alleys by yourself at night, I am just letting you know that these feelings and fears may crop up from time to time, however sad and probably unnecessary they might be. And the native Italians you are with may not fully understand them, which is probably for the best.

Note: I will also say, though, that this American preparedness kept me from having my money stolen in Venice once. Someone came up in a crowd and bumped me, and I felt them pick my pocket (Italy may have lower violent crime rates, but in touristy areas, pickpockets — usually not Italians, but other immigrants — are still a possibility). But all they got was my list of places I wanted to visit on our sightseeing trip because I had thought ahead and hid my cash in the inner lining of my jacket. So do with this information what you will.

27

Italians Take Their Dogs Everywhere

On a much happier note, there is one big bonus for dog lovers living in Italy: you can take your dog practically everywhere you go.

I don't believe there has been a single time that I have left my apartment and not seen at least three dogs keeping their humans company as they run errands or travel. And they don't just stay outside: you can bring your dog on the train, into most stores, and even into some restaurants! I don't have a dog at the moment (I have two cats!), but I am a bona fide dog person and I can't tell you how happy it makes me to see the smiling dogs out and about everywhere I go. Italians truly love their canine companions, and that makes me truly love them!

28

Keep Track of the Train Schedule

If you are going to be moving around at all in Italy, chances are, you're going to have to take the train. Aside from the people who travel by train to take sightseeing trips in a different region, millions of people take the train to work every day, or whenever they want to go to a different city (or even just a different place within their own city).

Unlike America's loud, diesel-fueled trains, Italy's trains run on electricity, and are usually quite comfortable. In terms of frequency of use and the convenience factor, they are almost the equivalent of taking the bus in America. People of all ages, races, and economic status take the train, making it a good place to really get a feel of all walks of Italian life.

An important tip: Keep your ticket handy at all times. Sometimes it seems like no one checks your ticket, but you never know when the *controllore* will come around to make sure you have one. And if you don't, you have to pay for one right then and there, plus an extra fee as a punishment. You can buy tickets ahead of time online, via an app, or through a clearly marked machine at the train station.

One other tip that is especially important for female train

riders is, if it is late at night and/or you are in an area where you don't feel safe (or you just don't want anyone to give you any sort of trouble, as, like I said, the train is a bit like the bus and therefore prone to being frequented by a few more "unsavory characters" late at night), sit in the first car of the train, just behind the conductor. This is the safest place on the train and no one will bother you here.

29

Cars Can Be Complicated

There is a widely held belief that Italians are bad drivers... but we'll get into that in a later section. For now, all you need to know is that, even if the steering wheel is on the same side of the car, you can't just hop into a car and Italy and start driving. The reason for this is that the large majority of cars here have a manual transmission, so if you don't know how to drive a stick shift, you are going to have problems.

And even if you do know how to drive a stick shift, you may also have issues when it comes time to fill up the tank. More and more cars are electric or hybrids these days, and some others use GPL as opposed to *benzina*, the type of gasoline we typically use. Some personal cars even use diesel, something that is mostly reserved for semi-trucks in America. So if you are renting a car, be sure to ask about all of these things before you get behind the wheel!

Okay, so you can drive a stick (or you found a car that's automatic and paid an arm and a leg to rent it) and you know what kind of fuel your car needs, so you're ready to hit the road, right? Wrong! There is one more thing you should know: the speed limit signs are in kilometers per hour (kph), not miles per hour (mph). This isn't really a big deal if you are driving an Italian car because you can just make sure the number on your speedometer matches the number on the speed limit signs. But if you were able to bring over a car from America, you are going to have to do some conversions, because there is a big difference between 50 miles per hour and 50 kilometers per hour (Hint: the former is faster)!

We discuss both driving and measurements in other sections, but for now, you should be ready to get behind the wheel... as long as you drive safely and understand the Italian road signs!

30
Watch Out for Bicyclists

This is one thing that both the United States and Italy have in common. Bicyclists usually ride in the same lanes as the vehicle traffic, so you really have to watch out for them when you are driving. Just like in America, most bike riders weave in and out of traffic, and a lot of them don't wear reflective gear at night, so it is a pretty dangerous situation for everyone involved if you aren't aware.

While this is surely a problem in the United States, it is a bigger one in Italy, because Italians on average are more environmentally conscious. This means that more people are riding bicycles to try to keep the air clean... but also that there are more of them in the road to slow down traffic or cause issues because everyone keeps trying to pass them (this isn't necessarily their fault, bikes are just slower than cars).

Riding a bike yourself is a great way to get exercise too (and to "go green"), so I'm not discouraging you or anyone else from doing it. I am just warning both parties to be very careful and to always watch out for each other.

31
Bars Are Not (Usually) for Alcohol

Now that you know how to get around, you can start going places. One popular place to visit is the bar, but be advised that Americans and Italians have different ideas about what the word "bar" means. In America, a bar is a place to drink alcohol and dance and maybe do karaoke. In Italy, it is a place to drink coffee and maybe eat a brioche.

Bars are open most of the day in Italy and are typically peaceful, relaxed places where you can order an espresso, which most people drink standing right there at the counter, or a snack like a slice of *focaccia* or a *granita*, a cold Sicilian dessert that is similar to a slushie, but more delicate.

If you are interested in the nightlife, though, you are looking for a "pub" (although some bars do sell alcohol as well). I tell you this so that if someone asks you at 9:00 am if you want to go to the bar, you don't accuse them of being an alcoholic or go put on your skimpiest miniskirt and expect a morning martini!

32

Here's a Tip: Don't Tip

"What? Are you crazy?" you ask. "Not tipping is like a slap in the face to the waiter or waitress! It's beyond rude!"

In America, maybe.

In recent years, the expected tip percentage has been increasing in leaps and bounds in the hospitality industry, but not in Italy. In America, you tip because the waiter or waitress is paid less than minimum wage, and a large part of their salary depends on the money they earn from tips.

In Italy, waiters, waitresses, and other hospitality workers are paid a steady, livable wage, and thusly don't expect tips. The same goes for delivery people — the tip is usually built into the price you pay for a meal or other service, so it isn't necessary to pay them anything extra.

In some countries like Japan, it is seen as outright rude to tip someone for doing their job. In Italy, you can try to tip them if you want or if they did a truly spectacular job, but they will surely find it a bit odd and may not even accept it because they feel that they are just doing what their job normally entails. Some restaurants may have a tip jar on the counter, but this isn't really the norm either.

Gratitude is always appreciated, though, so if you want to give a waiter or delivery person something extra, thank them sincerely and let them know how happy you are with the service they provided.

33

Sales Tax Isn't So Taxing Here

This is one of my favorite things about shopping in Italy: the price you see on the sticker is the price you pay for items you see in a store.

In America, there is almost always a sales tax added to the price of the stuff you buy, but it isn't added until the cashier rings it up. With this system, you don't really know for sure what anything will cost until you get to the register (or carry a calculator and/or do mental math the whole time you're shopping), which can be a bit stressful for those of us who aren't mathematically inclined.

In Italy, there is an IVA (*Imposta sul Valore Aggiunto*, their version of a sales tax) that is added into the price of some items, but it is added before you ever get to the store. The number you see on the price tag in the grocery or at the mall already includes any added taxes, therefore you always know exactly how much you are going to pay. So unless there is a discount you didn't know about, there are no surprises in the check-out lane!

Part III:
If You're Sick

Got the sniffles? Ate something bad? Broke an arm?
Here is a quick and simple guide to Italian healthcare, so you
know where to go when you need some looking after.

34

Which Doctor Do I Need?

Good news: Italy has free healthcare! This is a big part of what Italians pay for when they pay their taxes, so health services (even for expats who haven't gotten their health insurance card, the *Tessera Sanitaria,* yet) are free or very low-cost.

So, if you get hurt or are under the weather while you're under the Tuscan (or Venetian, or Sicilian, or Sardinian, or Milan-ian...) sun, you don't have to worry about how much a doctor's visit will cost you. The only thing you *do* have to worry about is figuring out which type of doctor to see. Here is a broad, general look at the different types of health care available:

- *Medico di base (or medico di famiglia)* - If you are an official Italian resident, this should be your go-to doctor. A *medico di base* or *medico di famiglia* is (literally, in the latter case) the family doctor, and you should go to yours for general consultations, physicals, and exams. If you are sick, they can prescribe medications, or they can send you to the right place to get an x-ray, ultrasound, or whatever else may help diagnose your condition. Like most doctor's offices in America, they are only open during normal business hours.

- **Pronto soccorso** - *Pronto soccorso* is basically the Italian equivalent of our emergency room. go here if you have a broken bone, heart attack, stroke, or any other very serious, very urgent medical issue. You can also go here outside of the regular business hours, unlike the *medico di base.*

- **Guardia medica** - *Guarda medica* is similar to what we would call an "urgent care center" in America. It is a substitute for a family doctor, and you can go here after business hours are over, during the weekends, or if your regular doctor is just out of the office for some reason.

- **Guardia turistica** - *Guardia turistica* is the same as *guardia medica*, but it caters specifically to people who are visiting Italy and/or don't have permanent residency. Even though it is for people whose home country probably wouldn't do the same, treatment here is usually free or low-cost.

- **Pediatra** - A *pediatra* is a pediatrician, so this is where you would take your children if they get ill or hurt. They are typically the same as the family doctor, but they specialize in children's health and can also tell you whether your little one is on the right track in terms of height, weight, and other factors.

This is, of course, not a comprehensive list of all the specialties that exist, but it should at least give you a good idea of where you need to go for most common medical problems.

35

You Can Take Your Prescription to Any Pharmacy

More good news: you know how in America you can only get your prescriptions filled at a pharmacy that's in your insurance network? Here, you don't have to worry about that.

In Italy, you can take your prescription to any pharmacy you want and they will fill it for you. Usually, you have to put in the order and come back later to pick it up, but this isn't a big deal. And there is practically a pharmacy on every corner, so you won't have any trouble finding one.

Two things to note, though:

1. Yes, there are pharmacies on every corner, but they all have different hours. Some are only open in the morning, others only in the afternoon, and some are just not open on Mondays for some reason that I have yet to figure out. But, when one is closed, there is usually another one open nearby, so you can just walk or drive down the street to find another. They are designed in such a way that you can always find an open pharmacy regardless of the time of day, you just may have to do a bit of looking.

2. Pharmacies in Italy are not like Walgreens or CVS or Rite Aid, all of which usually have aisles and aisles of things like overpriced makeup, toys, groceries, photo developing stations, and knick-knacks to give your mom as a last-minute Mother's Day gift. Italian pharmacies are just pharmacies: they have medicines and maybe some overpriced menstrual pads for the ladies, but that's it. So if you need a can of chicken soup or some magazines to go with your cold medicine, you won't find them there.

Cool Stuff

As if you need any more reasons to visit Italy...

This section is not so much tips as just really neat stuff I have observed and that you won't want to miss out on (and one thing that will save you a lot of money!).

36

You Can Go from the Sea
to 10,000 Meters in Minutes

Just like America, Italy has some really spectacular sights to see, making it the perfect place for a road trip. In Sicily, for example, you can go from sea level to the top of a snow-covered mountain (or even a snow-covered volcano!) in a matter of just a few minutes. There are so many different landscapes all mixed together, making it seem like you are seeing three or more different countries all at the same time.

Another cool thing about Italy is that, unlike in America, where you can drive for nine hours and still not have reached the end of your state (I'm looking at you, Texas), you can pass from one region to another — or even to another country like Switzerland — in just a matter of a few hours or less. And that's without taking an airplane! Italy is a great place to embrace your wanderlust, because you can really see a lot in one day.

37

You Can Practically
Have a Volcano in Your Backyard

While there are a few volcanoes here and there in America, there are a lot in Italy — and many of them are active. Some of them are constantly rumbling, occasionally emitting a few bursts of lava or sparks or smoke every now and then, and some of them just stand there quietly, reminding visitors that much of what they see of the Italian landscape is not just hundreds, but hundreds of *thousands* of years old.

What is interesting, though, is that many people visit these volcanoes on a daily basis. They just pack a lunch and go hiking up Mount Etna on a Saturday afternoon like it couldn't erupt at any moment, which, to be honest, seems pretty badass to an outsider. Volcanoes are almost just like mountains in Italy: they are just another part of the land, and many people live right at the foot of them with no fear.

38

Italy Is a Land of Myths and Legends

Roman Mythology has always been endlessly fascinating, even to people with no interest in Italy. It becomes even more fascinating when you are able to visit the places referenced in the epic tales of gods and heroism, and where the legends were literally born.

Historically, Romans used myths to describe how their culture came to be and how their religion was formed. There were Romulus and Remus, for example, twin brothers who were breastfed by a wolf and founded the city of Rome. There were gods and goddesses like Janus, Vesta, Jupiter, and Apollo who each represented a different aspect of Roman/Italian culture, and there are dozens of stories about how these and other gods had secret (or not-so-secret) affairs with humans that either led to important figures being born, or to various historical events occurring. Basically, Romans used mythology to understand the world around them, and that mythology was passed down through the centuries to the extent that we can still study it in school today, even half a world away.

It makes sense that the source of Roman myths like these can be found in Italy, because it was where the great Roman

Empire began its spread (you should read up on these things if you have a chance — it is very interesting but it would make this book ten times longer if I went into detail on it here). But you may also be surprised to learn that many *Greek* myths and legends have origins in Italy as well.

Mount Etna is said to be where Hephaestus, the Greek god of fire (referred to as Vulcan by the Romans), made his fiery home and did his blacksmithing work. The Aeolian Islands were named after the Greek god of wind, Aeolus, and are where Odysseus went after he fought the Cyclops in Homer's *The Odyssey*. And this is just the beginning. Sicily alone is home to countless myths and legends, which I will go into much more detail on in my next book for those who are interested!

The thing you need to know, though, is that to walk in Italy is to walk the same streets as gods and heroes who were said to live thousands of years ago. Pretty cool, huh?

39

Firefighting Looks Fun

Now we move onto something more modern, but still fascinating.

Fires are never a good thing. But if you are staying in a region near the sea, a fire could give you the opportunity to see something kind of awesome.

In Italy, firefighters don't always just spray water from a hose on their truck, and they don't have to struggle to try to get into a tight spot in the woods if it goes up in flames. Instead, there are helicopters and planes (the latter are called Canadair) that scoop up water from the sea and use that water to put out the fire.

Depending on the aircraft, it either uses something that looks like a basket and drags it in the water, filling it up, or it just skims the surface of the water like a dragonfly and pulls the water into a compartment in the plane or helicopter itself. Then it flies back to the site of the fire and the pilot pushes a button, releasing the totally natural, totally free water. Then it goes back and starts the whole process again, and continues until the fire is extinguished.

I can't tell you how many kids and adults alike — even those who have lived in Italy all their lives — I've seen sitting outside, watching the firefighters work. And I don't blame them, it's really neat!

40

Phone Plans Are *MUCH* Cheaper

The rest of the items in this section are mostly about sights you can see and things you can do, but this one is something practical... and also a bit of a sore spot with me!

In America, there is really no such thing as a "cheap" phone plan. Some companies charge you $15 per month, but only if you pay for an entire year at once. Others think $35 per month with no data and just a handful of minutes is a good deal. But let me tell you about Italian phone plans.

Here, you can find a plan that includes all the bells and whistles (data, unlimited minutes, unlimited texts, etc.) for eight to ten euros a month. That's less than ten or twelve dollars! But I'm not finished. Those plans are considered the expensive ones: most people pay around *two* euros per month for a plan with two gigabytes of data and a few hundred minutes. So, like, three dollars! For more than most people would even need!!

I sincerely thought my husband was pulling my leg when he told me that his phone plan costs only €2.50 per month. I had been paying $35 in the States and I had had to buy data as an add-on for an additional $5 every month! It seemed impossible that phone plans could be so cheap... but when I started looking into getting my own Italian phone number, I saw that it was true. And I am still kind of furious about it... But it's good news for those who want to buy an Italian SIM card to use when you come to live or visit!

41

The Best Places to Visit Aren't the Tourist Attractions

I have been to Rome to see the Colosseum and the Trevi Fountain. I have seen the painting on the ceiling of the Sistine Chapel. I have been to Venice to see the canals. I have been to Florence to see the statue of David and the stunning vistas, and I have been to Verona to see the place where Shakespeare's famous balcony scene in *Romeo and Juliet* was set. I have been to most of the big, popular tourist attractions in Italy, and they were pretty great.

But they were nothing compared to the places that *aren't* on the list of most popular destinations.

Sicily, for example, where my husband is from, is not very well-traveled by those coming from abroad, and this is a real shame. Sicily has some of the most absolutely incredible natural sights I have ever seen, ranging from the beaches and the sea to the mountains and volcanoes I mentioned earlier. Even in Rome, the best thing I saw was a park full of statues and greenery that was almost completely devoid of visitors, and the coolest thing about Venice was a little museum that's barely noticeable to passersby walking down the street.

You of course should see the big touristy sites, but mostly just because it is really thrilling to say that you saw something you had only previously seen in a book. But there is another reason why I prefer the less-charted places. The truth is (and I don't want to disappoint you, but maybe it's better to hear it from me first, since I wish someone had told me), the touristy places are usually kind of annoying to visit, because they are flooded with people who think that these are the only things to see in the entire country.

I had been waiting my whole life to see that Sistine Chapel ceiling, having pored over pictures of it in books for years. But when I actually got there, ready to soak in all the grandeur, I was really disappointed. And bored. And hot. To get to the chapel where the painting is, you have to traverse the entire Vatican Museum, which takes hours. It is full of signs saying things like, "Just three more rooms until you get to the Sistine Chapel," "Just two more rooms until you get to the Sistine Chapel," "Just ten more rooms until you get to the Sistine Chapel!" (I swear this happened). The closer you get to the thing you actually came to see, the further away it feels, and the more crowded it gets. The rooms were packed, the lines didn't move for hours, there was no air conditioning, and finally, *finally*, when I got to the actual chapel, there were so many people pushing and shoving and just trying to make space for themselves that I barely gave the darn ceiling a cursory glance before I was ready to leave.

The Trevi Fountain was the same: we had to fight our way through the crowd to get close enough to toss in a coin, and by the time we made it, I was so frustrated by the rude tourists and the guys hawking selfie-sticks and overpriced souvenirs that I couldn't even really enjoy it.

I still got some beautiful pictures that I can look back on with pride and fondness while I say "I was really there," but in the end, the places I enjoy the most are always off the beaten path. Italy has so much more to offer than what you see on the tourism websites or in travel books, and you don't want to miss out on it because it's not perpetually trending on social media.

I Shouldn't Have to Say This, But...

There are a lot of Italian stereotypes out there, just like there are a lot of (usually offensive) American ones. I shouldn't have to tell you that they're not true... but for the sake of the Italians you'll be interacting with, I will.

42

Not Everything Is Set to the Tune of a Mandolin

You've heard it before: every time someone in a movie or on a television show goes to Italy, instantly the soundtrack changes to the same, stereotypical song. You probably can't name said song (I couldn't, but I just found out that a large portion of the time it's a song called "Tarantella Napoletana" and was first played at the end of a comic opera by a composer from Naples named Luigi Ricci in the 1800s if you want to look it up), but you know the one I mean. And whenever you hear it, you think of Italy, because that's what you've been conditioned to do.

But I'm here to tell you that Italians *hate* that song. Or, more accurately, they hate that people in other countries believe that the only type of music they have here is that goofy-sounding song or something else played on the mandolin. So don't expect to hear that tune here, and definitely don't ask anyone to play it.

43

Not Everyone Has Mustache

Or a dark complexion. Or dark hair. There is a tendency for people to think that Italians are all olive-skinned brunettes, but in actuality, there are almost as many different hair colors and skin types in Italy as there are in America. There are natural blondes and natural redheads, pale people, dark-skinned people, freckles... the list goes on and on. And the reason for this is because Italians can trace their heritage back to a huge number of different ethnic groups. Their history goes back much farther than ours (I'm talking B.C., so thousands of years), and includes immigration and/or conquering from groups as diverse as the Phoenicians, Greeks, and Arabs, in addition to the Romans, who spread their empire throughout the whole country.

Note: To be completely historically accurate, I must make a note that these outside conquering influences influenced the southern parts of Italy, such as the island of Sicily, the most, so the north may be slightly less varied in terms of genealogy. But still, the takeaway here is that Italy's population is not just one big homogeneous group of "Italians." In reality, its roots spread far and wide, making it almost as big of a melting pot as America!

44

Not Everyone Is into Fashion
and Cars Either

Obviously, Milan is famous for its fashion week and Fiat is one of the most famous car producers in the world, but Italy isn't *just* high fashion and fast driving. You don't have to feel like you are under-dressed if you aren't wearing a designer label, and you don't have to drive a sports car to be cool. Those are just two small things that come from this country, they aren't representative of the country as a whole. Not everyone is into talking about the latest trends in vehicles *or* shoes, so don't use those things as your go-to icebreaker unless you know the person you are talking to is interested in them.

Trust me, there are plenty of average, unfashionable people here driving hoopties, just like in the U.S.!

As with the previous item on this list, there is a tendency to over-generalize when it comes to our ideas about Italians and their culture. But in reality, Italy is full of diverse people with diverse interests that you will never get to know unless you let go of the stereotypes society has taught us over the years.

45
Speaking of Cars...

Remember how I said that not everyone in Italy drives a sports car? Well, not everyone drives like a maniac either. This is a very pervasive stereotype seen in movies and t.v. shows, and to generalize something like that is always wrong.

But...

I have to admit that the style of driving in Italy actually does take some getting used to. While not everyone is driving on the sidewalks or parking wherever they want, it can sometimes seem like Italian drivers are going extra fast and doing more high-risk maneuvers than we are used to in the States.

A big part of this is due to the fact that Italian roads were built back when cars were smaller, so they are narrower than the roads in America. This makes it seem like the cars are much closer together and much closer to a collision than they maybe actually are. Often, there are cars parked on the sides of the road in some towns as well, bringing the driving space down to one lane. This means people have to try to pass other people to get by or juke suddenly to keep from hitting someone opening a door onto the street, so it can all feel a bit stressful if you're not used to it!

So, while I can't exactly say that the stereotype is completely unfounded (no offense to any native Italian readers!), I can also say that it is less "crazy driving" and more like "a style of driving we aren't accustomed to."

46

Mario and Luigi Are Kind of Offensive

Sure, it's fun to say "It's a-me! Mario!" in your best Super Mario accent, but most Italians will not appreciate that very much. To them, Mario and Luigi are not very good representations of Italian culture (although a lot of Italians still love playing their games, don't get me wrong). Apparently it's a bit of a groaner when you tell someone you're Italian and they automatically reply, "Oh, like Super Mario!", even if that someone might be doing it good-naturedly.

For one thing, Mario was actually created by a Japanese game company, not an Italian one, and for another thing, he's kind of just a bunch of Italian stereotypes personified. So please don't expect everyone to be running around in red overalls and sporting a cheesy mustache while they fix the pipes!

47

Italians Don't Say
"Mamma Mia!" All the Time
(and You Shouldn't Either!)

I just used it as an example in the last item, but I want to make sure it is clear that this is another big stereotype that really bugs most Italians. While "*Mamma mia*" *is* a phrase used to express shock or dismay, it isn't something people say a hundred times a day. And if you, someone from a different country who probably isn't using it right, try to say it, you're going to seem like you're making fun of them, which is just not cool.

Plus, it turns out that if you say something like "*Mamma mia, this is some good pizza!*" to your husband as a joke, he pulls a face and steals your last bite of dinner. So, learn from this (totally hypothetical... really...) example and keep your *Mamma mias* to yourself!

48

Not Everyone Is a Gangster

We've all seen *The Godfather* and, while it's a fine film franchise, it has given a lot of Americans the wrong idea about Italians. Sicilians, in particular. While it is true that the Mafia was a big deal back in the 19th and 20th centuries, it isn't very prevalent today, and the chances of you meeting someone involved in it or get caught up in it somehow yourself are slim to none.

Whether you think the Mafia is cool or whether it makes you nervous, it is rude to imply that any Italian you come across is in the mob. Just as we Americans don't like to constantly be reminded of the bad or violent things that happened in our country's past, Italians don't either. So just don't do it.

Fun fact: The history of the Mafia isn't black and white. We think of the Mafia as a criminal organization full of bad guys, but it was actually started as what almost amounts to a vigilante group that helped to fight off all of the different armies who were trying to invade and conquer Sicily. This eventually led to that group going out to shake people down and try to get them to pay them protection fees and things of that nature, though...

There were also times during which the Mafia helped law enforcement catch even more dangerous criminals than them, but this was in exchange for policemen looking the other way when they themselves did crimes... so, like I said, it's complicated. And this is another reason not to make snap/blanket judgments!

A Few More

Quick, Random Tips

This advice didn't fit into the other categories, but you'll still be glad you read it.

Learn from my experience. Avoid my mistakes!

49

Learn at Least a Bit of Italian

A lot of people believe that they can travel to a foreign country and not have to worry about knowing that country's language in order to get around. To a certain extent, this may be true in modern-day Italy, mostly in the more touristy areas, but that isn't really the point. Would you expect an Italian to come and visit and/or live in America without knowing any English at all? Without even trying?

No, because that is just disrespectful, and that is the sort of thing that leads to the all-too-pervasive stereotype of the "ugly American abroad."

While you don't have to be fluent, it is just good manners to at least try to learn a bit of Italian, especially if you are going to be spending a lot of time with native speakers. Your Italian may not be fantastic, but the fact that you're trying will impress a lot of people and make them enjoy your company even more. In my experience, most Italians are very helpful when it comes to speaking their language (and a lot of them know at least a bit of English because they take English courses in school here, unlike most of us who may not have had the opportunity to do the same with Italian), and they will be more than happy to bear with you as you try to practice communicating with them.

Note: If you're shy like I am, you won't be happy to know that the key to speaking Italian (or any other language) more fluently is confidence. But one tip I can give is that, if you are in it for the long haul and want to really master the Italian language, immersion is your best bet. Watch t.v. shows in Italian (with Italian subtitles — doing it with English subtitles is cheating!), read books in Italian, listen to Italian music, and most of all, speak to other Italian speakers. It will take some time and some effort to get comfortable with it, but you will be surprised at how good you can get in a short time!

50

Pronto? Is It Me You're Looking for?

In the United States, we are taught at a young age how to answer the phone, so we're pretty much experts. Everyone from the eighty-year-old woman who fields calls from her children and grandchildren every day to the teenagers who spend their nights gossiping with their friends to the two-year-old playing with a big, chunky red plastic phone toy with an outdated rotary dial knows exactly what to say when they answer the phone:

"Hello?"

So in Italy you'd think that you could just translate that to "ciao" and you'd be fine, right? Nope!

When you pick up a phone in Italy (especially if you see that it's an Italian number on your cell phone's caller ID), you don't say "hello," or "ciao," or anything of that nature. Instead, you say "*pronto*."

Pronto means "ready," and although its origins aren't crystal clear, it is thought to date back to the days of operators and switchboards. They would ask if someone was ready to receive a call, and the person would reply "*pronto*": "I'm ready."

It will take a bit of time to get used to this method of answering the phone, since we have all been saying "hello" since we were in diapers. But in the meantime, just know that if someone says "*pronto*" to you when they answer your call, they aren't being cold or pretending to be a spy waiting for their next piece of intel. They are just saying that they are ready to listen to what you have to say.

51

Don't Expect Everyone to Be on Time All the Time

In Italy, especially in the parts that are more like small towns and aren't so "citified," things move at their own pace. If someone has an appointment at 1:00, they might leave the house at 12:55 and get there a few minutes late, and no one says a word about it (and sometimes the other party is late too!). Times for get-togethers at other people's houses are more like guidelines than firm schedules, so someone may show up ten minutes early or fifteen minutes late without the need to call and tell anyone about it. It's not that Italians don't want to be punctual, it's just that, a lot of times, things are just more relaxed and the timings aren't always exact.

As nice as it might be to never have to worry about being a few minutes late, this was a tough thing for me to wrap my always-punctual head around (and I still haven't quite accepted it yet, to be honest). To me, if you're not half an hour early, you're late. But for my husband, being ready to leave the house more than half an hour before an appointment is just silly.

While I'm not recommending that you actively try to be late, I will caution you that not everyone will show up exactly on time, unless it is something very important like a work meeting or a doctor's appointment. Some Italians just won't be rushed, and as much as our American get-it-done-now mentality might want to speed things up, we just can't. We have to learn to go with the flow and have a bit of patience.

52

Your Money Is (Sometimes)
No Good Here

If you are planning a trip to Italy, you will already know that you are going to have to exchange some of your U.S. dollars for euros. What you may *not* know is that the value of those dollars changes all the time.

The first time I came to Italy, the exchange rate was basically one to one. My dollars were almost equal to the value of the euros, so I had no trouble doing exchanges and keeping track of how much I could spend.

Over the past four years, though, this exchange rate has not been favorable for Americans at all. I had no idea before that the exchange rate is affected by things like the stock market, which in turn is affected by things like, say, controversy in American politics or the presence of a certain worldwide epidemic. If America is having a bad time, the value of the dollar goes down, which is bad news for us expats looking to make an exchange.

Recently, for example, the exchange rate was down to around $0.85 for every €1. This means that, putting aside the fees that currency exchange companies always charge you, you have to pay $1.17 for every one euro you spend. While seventeen cents might not seem like it will break the bank, that change really adds up when you start paying for more expensive things!

Unfortunately, there isn't really much you can do about this, except maybe wait around a day or two (or a month or two...) to see if the rates improve before you do an exchange. There are many websites where you can check the exchange rate daily, such as xe.com and transferwise.com, and it is always a good idea to keep an eye on those.

53

Be Careful When You Write (and Read) the Date

This one can be very tricky! In America, we are used to writing the date Month/Day/Year. But in Italy, the format is different: Day/Month/Year. It goes from the smallest time increment (a day) to the biggest time increment (a year), if that helps you to remember, but you really have to get a handle on this if you don't want to run into trouble. Reading expiration dates on items at the grocery store, for instance, can be problematic if you read 10/8/2020 as October 8, 2020, instead of as August 10, 2020, and you can totally miss a concert if you read 5/4/2020 as May 4th instead of April 5th!

Most Italians also use the 24-hour clock instead of the 12-hour one (5:00 pm would be 17:00, for instance), but seeing as most people here understand the time either way you say it (and you'll know that 17 is later than 5 if you read it somewhere), this is not nearly as problematic.

The date format, though, is a must-learn if you don't want to drink expired milk or be super late for a date!

54

Expand Your Stomach

If you learn nothing else from this book, learn this: your American stomach is not ready for the sheer volume of food you will eat in Italy, trust me! As I said in the Food and Drink section, Italians eat multiple courses per meal, and each course is almost equivalent to one full meal back home. So you're going to want to slowly but surely try to expand your stomach before you come so that you can pack it all in when you get here!

While no one will be upset with you if you don't finish your plate due to getting full early, I can't tell you how many times I have been teased thanks to my "small American stomach!" It was all in good fun of course (even if it was very strange to hear someone call an American stomach "small" with all the not-so-nice American stereotypes floating around), but I will admit that it is a bit sad to see everyone else eating heaping portions of delicious food after you've already reached capacity.

So, if you can, try to expand your stomach before you come so you don't miss out on the opportunity to eat as much as possible!

Ciao

In Italian, "*ciao*" means both "hello" and "goodbye."
Now it is time to say goodbye to you, but hopefully time for
you to say hello to some newfound confidence in your Italian
adventures!

55

A Kiss Hello and a Kiss Goodbye

Before we say goodbye, there is one last thing I want to tell you about how to be an American in Italy, and it is a bit bittersweet at the moment.

In Italy, you don't just say "hi" or "bye" with a handshake or a wave. People who know each other (both male and female) typically greet one another with a kiss. To do this, you simply place your cheek against the other person's cheek, do an air-kiss (don't actually put your lips on their face unless you *really* know them), then repeat on the other cheek. In Italy in general, you do one kiss per cheek, but in some places you repeat the process twice or even three times.

It is a nice, personal little custom that makes you instantly feel warm and fuzzy and closer to people. But, unfortunately, it can't be carried out much in the COVID-19 era during which I am writing this book. This makes a lot of Italians feel very sad and lost when it comes time to say hello or goodbye to the people they care about because, for them, a wave or a smile without a hug and a kiss just doesn't cut it. They want to show their fondness, their love, and their care for others, but they are forced to hold themselves back. It is really heartbreaking to see, even if it's not a custom that most

Americans are used to back home.

So, if you didn't already have enough of a reason to be safe and do your part in making the world a better place in 2020/2021 (and every year), do it for the Italians who just want to show their affection to you and their loved ones!

My parting advice to those of you already living in, visiting, or moving to Italy is to try everything: taste every food, test out every custom, visit every place you can, especially those not listed in your travel books. Italy has so much to offer you and, as Americans, we have our own unique way of experiencing it and sharing in it that no one else has.

Hopefully soon the world will heal, people will be able to travel more, and you will be able to put the tips in this book into practice. One day we Americans in Italy can meet up and greet each other with a kiss on the cheek, or maybe even bring this lovely custom back with us to our hometowns in the U.S.

Until then, *ciao*!

Grazie per aver letto!
(Thanks for reading)

I have really enjoyed writing this book, and I hope you have enjoyed reading it. Thank you so much for picking it up, and I hope it helps you to feel more at home in Italy, however long you choose to stay.

I'd love to hear your feedback! If you could leave a quick review (even one or two lines is great!) on Amazon or other retailers' websites, it would really help this book get noticed and help me to improve future projects.

For even more tips (and a **free quick-reference guide**) you can sign up to join the An American in Italy mailing list at **www.anamericaninitaly.com**, where you can also check out my weekly blog posts on everything from food to language to the always "ugh"-inducing Italian bureaucracy.

Thanks again for reading.
Arrivederci!

About the Author

Jessica Scott Romano has been writing since she was three years old. Born in Louisville, Kentucky, she graduated from the University of Louisville with degrees in English and Humanities. Her concentrations included Literature, Linguistics, and Classical and Modern languages, all of which expanded her mind and took her to places she never thought she would go. After reading far too many books about grand adventures in faraway places, she was inspired to go on a few of her own. She now lives in Italy with her husband and two cats, where she spends her days writing, traveling, and sampling every delicious dish the country has to offer.

To learn about her novels and other non-fiction work, visit her website at www.jessicascottromano.com.

Made in the USA
Las Vegas, NV
20 March 2022